DODD, MEAD WONDERS BOOKS include WONDERS OF:

The Wonders of Flightless Birds

Sigmund A. Lavine

Illustrated with photographs and old prints

DODD, MEAD & COMPANY, NEW YORK

Illustrations courtesy of: American Museum of Natural History, 45, 46, 51; Australian News and Information Bureau, 64, 66; Field Museum of Natural History, Chicago, 14, 20, 23, 26, 28, 36, 39, 42, 60, 71, 72, 77; Mike Kops, *frontispiece;* Theodore K. Mason, 47, 49, 50; National Publicity Studios, Wellington, New Zealand, 8, 68, 69; New Zealand Embassy *(Evening Post),* 82, 83, 84; New Zealand Information Service, 19, 32, 33, 34, 35, 37; Jane O'Regan, 29; South African Tourist Corporation, 54–55, 56, 58, 59, 62.

Frontispiece: Close-up of head of an ostrich

1 2 3 4 5 6 7 8 9 10

Library of Congress Catalog in Publication Data

Lavine, Sigmund A.
  Wonders of flightless birds.

  Includes index.
  Summary: Discusses the first bird, extinct birds including the roc, great auk, and dodo, and forty-six living species of birds that lack the power of flight.
  1. Birds—Juvenile literature. 2. Birds, Extinct—Juvenile literature. [1. Birds. 2. Extinct birds]
  I. Title.
  QL676.2.L38   598   81–43236
  ISBN 0–396–08003–0   AACR2

For Corrine, who makes no attempt to clip Bill's wings

Contents

The kiwi of New Zealand, a living flightless bird

1 History of Birds

"Nature's mightiest law is change."—Burns

The First Bird

In 1861, a workman splitting slate in a Bavarian quarry uncovered the fossil of a feathered animal. Sold to the British Museum in London, the fossil was studied by some of the leading scientists of the day. These experts named it *Archaeopteryx lithographica*—"the ancient creature of the stone for drawing."

Examination of the fossil—and of similar ones found in 1871 and 1956—revealed that *Archaeopteryx* had many of the physical characteristics of the reptiles that inhabited the Earth some 150 million years ago. But despite toothed jaws, reptile-like bone structure, and a long, bony, lizard-like tail, ornithologists—students of bird life—classify *Archaeopteryx* as a bird. They have good reason. All the fossil specimens reveal that, while *Archaeopteryx* had many reptilian features, it possessed physical characteristics found only in birds. These include a unique arrangement of certain hipbones and a wishbone formed by the joining of the collarbones. Moreover, the fossils have remarkably clear imprints of feathers on each side of the tail and on the wings. Paleontologists are agreed that the structure of *Archaeopteryx'* feathers was identical to those of modern birds. The experts are also positive that the fossilized feathers were attached to the wings in the same fashion as are the feathers of many living species. As a result, there is no doubt that the fossils are those of birds.

To date, *Archaeopteryx* is the oldest known bird. There may have been earlier ones. Actually, it is impossible to trace completely the history of birds. This is due to the lack of fossil evidence. Not only have very few birds died under conditions suitable for fossilization but also most bird bones are small and easily broken—"few of them have been preserved in the record of the rocks."

Ornithologists theorize that the immediate forebears of *Archaeopteryx* and all other birds were lizards that had adapted to living in trees, where they used their tails as balancers and their legs for climbing and hanging. Over the centuries, the scales on the forelimbs evolved into feathers that enabled the

Old print identified as Ramphorynchus. *Ornithologists theorize that birds evolved from lizards.*

A fossil of Archeopteryx. *Specimen from Solenhofen, studied by Owen.*

lizards to jump farther, glide longer distances, and make parachute-like landings. Eventually, the lizards developed feathered wings and learned to fly.

The crow-sized *Archaeopteryx* probably spent considerable time in trees because fossils reveal that its toes were modified for perching. Undoubtedly, *Archaeopteryx'* ability to fly was limited. Fossil imprints of its breastbone show that this ancient bird had to be a weak flyer because not only were the wings insignificant and rounded but also they were powered by small muscles. Therefore it is very likely that *Archaeopteryx* employed its wings more for gliding than for flying. It appears that *Archaeopteryx* was capable of rising flight when moving from branch to branch, but the chances are it did considerable climbing because each of its forelimbs had three claw-equipped fingers that would insure a firm grip on limbs and bark.

Paleontologists who specialize in bird fossils have determined that *Archaeopteryx* could not change direction quickly or perform other maneuvers in the air because its cerebellum—the part of the brain that controls muscular activity—was small. Another reason why *Archaeopteryx* was not a skilled flyer is that it lacked the slender, hollow bones that modern birds possess.

However, the various flying reptiles that inhabited the same forests as the first known bird did have this adaptation for lightness.

Other "Early Birds"

During the Cretaceous Period, which began about 135 million years ago and lasted some 70 million years, a huge inland sea covered present-day Kansas. Chalk deposits left by its waters contain fossils that show birds were evoluting slowly into their present-day form as well as becoming highly specialized.

The best-known fossil birds found in Cretaceous rocks are *Ichthyornis,* the "fish bird," and *Hesperornis,* the "western bird." *Ichthyornis,* a ternlike bird about eight inches tall, was a strong flyer. On the other hand, six-foot-long *Hesperornis* was incapable of flight because its wings were rudimentary. An accomplished diver with large, powerful legs adapted for swimming, *Hesperornis,* like its reptilian ancestors, had toothed jaws.

By the end of the Cretaceous Period, many modern bird families were established. Fossil evidence also provides proof that

A drawing of Hesperornis *swimming, based on museum skeletons*

12

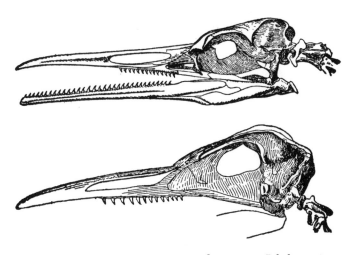

Skulls of, TOP, Hesperornis, *and* BOTTOM, Ichthyornis

many of the bird families known today came into being with the passing of the centuries. While the vast majority of these birds relied on their wings for locomotion, some, like *Hersperornis*, were content with an aquatic life. Others inhabited isolated islands where, free from predators, they had no need of flight. Still others, like the diatrymids of Europe and North America, were too big and too heavy to fly. Powerful birds, the diatrymids stood seven feet tall. Their skulls, which were as large as those of horses, bore huge hooked beaks.

The diatrymids became extinct long before man appeared on Earth. However, man is responsible for the annihilation of several species of flightless birds through thoughtless predation and by interference with the balance of nature. Presently, man-induced extinction threatens a small flock of flightless birds. If these birds vanish, the lesson hidden in the stories of the species that have disappeared will be ignored. Hopefully, this will not happen.

Remains of the elephant bird found in Madagascar reveal that it became extinct in historical time. Thus this flightless giant may be responsible for the legend of the roc.

2 Some Extinct Flightless Birds

"Dead as the dodo."—Proverbial saying

The Roc

Marco Polo, returning to Venice in 1294 after his long stay at Kublai Khan's court, visited the island of "Magastar." While there, he heard of the roc, a native bird so big and strong that it could "seize an elephant in its talons. . . . and eat him at leisure."

Marco Polo did not see the roc. But, according to the *Thousand and One Nights*, Sinbad the Sailor landed on an island during his second voyage and found a roc's egg "fifty paces in diameter."

Without doubt, both "Magastar" and Sinbad's island were Madagascar, which lies east of Africa. Proof of this is furnished by the logs of Arab traders who went to Madagascar during the early Middle Ages. They tell of a huge bird they encountered there.

The Arab seamen were not spinning a yarn to enthrall landlubbers. When Etienne de Flacourt, the first French governor of Madagascar, published his *History of the Great Island of Madagascar* in 1658, he described the vouronpatra, "a giant bird that lays eggs as big as those of an ostrich."

Old print shows natives filling their elephant-bird eggshells and water-skins at a desert pool.

More than two centuries passed before anything further was heard of this ostrich-like bird. Then, in the mid-nineteenth century, travelers and merchants began sending enormous eggs back to Europe from Madagascar. Along with the eggs went accounts of how the natives of that island used the shells of similar eggs as vessels.

When museum authorities examined the eggs, they were amazed. Each egg was more than a foot long, weighed nearly thirty pounds, and had a capacity of about two gallons. This is the equivalent of 7 ostrich eggs, 180 chicken eggs, or 12,000 hummingbird eggs!

16

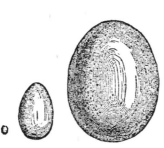

Comparative size of eggs, left to right: hummingbird, chicken, ostrich, and Aepyornis *or elephant bird*

After examining some eggs and a few bones, the director of the Paris zoo came to the conclusion that a large, flightless, ostrich-like bird was, or had been, native to Madagascar. He called it *Aepyornis maximus,* which can be translated "the tallest of the tall birds." The choice of name was an excellent one. In 1866, a complete skeleton of *Aepyornis* was unearthed. It revealed that the roc of legend stood between nine and ten feet tall and weighed close to a thousand pounds. This is why *Aepyornis* is popularly known as the elephant bird.

While several nineteenth-century expeditions failed to find a living roc or elephant bird, fossil discoveries showed that there had been nine species of Aepyornithids. Even today elephant bird eggs are dug out of the muck near lakes or washed out of the soil in Madagascar. Some eggs still contain the bones of unhatched chicks.

Although man deprived the elephant bird of nesting sites by cutting down Madagascar's forests, he is not entirely responsible for its extinction. A few centuries ago, Madagascar's climate underwent a drastic change. The resulting decrease in the annual rainfall caused many of the swamps in which *Aepyornis* had lived to disappear. Unable to adjust to a new environment, the elephant bird or roc of legend vanished.

Moa

Professor Richard Owen knew that the splintered and battered bone a friend had sent him from New Zealand in 1839 was a thighbone. But Owen, England's leading authority on ancient animals, had no idea to what creature it belonged. By comparing the femur with the thighbones of various animals, Owen found that the New Zealand bone was similar to an ostrich's thighbone. This discovery prompted Owen to announce at a meeting of the London Zoological Society held in November, 1839, that

18

Reconstruction shows Polynesian hunters attacking the giant moa. Formerly, twenty-five species of moa ranging in size from specimens fourteen feet tall to the small bush moa that stood about three feet high roamed the open country of New Zealand. These birds were a valuable source of food for the Polynesian settlers, and this finally brought about their extinction.

he was positive New Zealand was the home of a large and probably flightless bird, "nearly, if not quite, equal in size to the ostrich."

Owen's declaration prompted a search for the great bird the natives of New Zealand, the Maori, called the moa. None was

19

By studying the fossilized remains of moas and drawing on Maori lore, Charles Knight painted this picture of a flock of moas in New Zealand before it was settled by Europeans.

found, but a great number of fossilized and unfossilized moa bones were discovered. Owen reconstructed the moa with some of these bones and gave the bird the scientific name *Dinornis* (terrible bird). Owen's research led him to believe that there were five species of moa. He was wrong. Today we know that there were twenty-odd species. The largest was twelve feet tall; the smallest no bigger than a turkey.

Because bits of skin and feathers have been found near the complete skeletons of different species of moa, we know how the living birds looked. Scientists have also determined what moas ate. Specimens found in a swamp were so well preserved that the contents of their stomachs could be identified and moas classified as herbivorous.

Actually, the only mystery about the moa is the time at which it became extinct. Even as late as the mid-nineteenth century, elderly Maori were claiming they had hunted the bird in their youth. If they did, their prey must have been one of the smaller species. Fossils subjected to modern scientific techniques show that *Dinornis* vanished about A.D. 1500 and its various kin be-

Old print of Dinornis, *the terrible bird. The small birds at the moa's feet appear to be kiwis.*

came extinct between two and three hundred years ago. Nevertheless, every so often it is rumored that a moa has been sighted. But it is extremely unlikely that a moa of any size still exists. Indeed, it is astonishing that the moa survived as long as it did. The moa-hunting culture of the Maori doomed the bird to extinction. Not only did these tribesmen eat moa's flesh and eggs but also "they adorned their hair with the feathers, crushed the skulls and tattooed themselves with the powder, made fish hooks from the bones, and placed the giant eggs with the dead in their graves."

Great Auk

During the sixteenth and seventeenth centuries, the hardy men who fished the coastal waters of the North Atlantic islands in dories amused themselves by trying to overtake a swimming great auk *(Pinquinus impennis)*. They never did. An outstanding swimmer, the flightless great auk clove the water at high speed by employing its greatly reduced wings as flippers and by kicking with its broad feet. Great auks were not only capable of swimming rapidly but also had tremendous endurance. *Impennis* could take deep dives. This ability made it almost impossible for even an expert marksman to bag a great auk in the water— the bird invariably was beneath the surface long before the bullet could reach it.

But no bird was more clumsy on land than the great auk. About two feet tall, with legs set so far back on the body that it had to stand upright, *impennis* tottered as it waddled along and, to keep its balance, waved its flippers up and down.

Prehistoric man—who hunted only on land—had no difficulty killing the great auk. Remains of these birds have been found at the sites of ancient settlements in places as far apart as the

Once numerous in subarctic and temperate waters throughout the world, the great auk became extinct in 1844 when the last known pair of these birds was killed.

Atlantic Coast of North America and Russia. The number of auk bones unearthed in kitchen middens and other refuse dumps is tremendous. Therefore, it is logical to assume that there were once untold thousands of great auks in the subarctic and temperate waters of the world. However, man's predations over the centuries rapidly reduced the great auk population. Approximately a thousand years ago, the bird became extinct throughout much of its former range in the Old World.

However, the explorers who sailed along the northeastern coast of the New World and the fishermen who followed them found huge colonies of great auks in Labrador, Newfoundland, and on many small islands.

The great auks of the New World became the major source of food for seafarers, who clubbed them to death by the thousands. Besides being eaten fresh, auks were salted and stored in barrels for future use. In addition to salting down the bird flesh, the settlers of Newfoundland used the feathers to stuff mattresses, rendered fuel and lamp oil from the fat, and made fishhooks from the bones. They also baited their hooks with auk meat.

Great auks were slaughtered while nesting in summer—the only season they remained on land. Killing the birds before they hatched their yellowish-white, black, and brown speckled eggs—which were considered a delicacy—resulted in fewer and fewer great auks being born each year. Eventually, the large flocks vanished and only a few great auks could be found on scattered, inaccessible islands. When museum curators and private collectors—the individuals who should have tried to aid the birds—heard that the great auk was vanishing, they began to pay hundreds of dollars for auk skins and auk eggs.

No one knows how much three fishermen were paid for the bodies of the two great auks they killed on tiny Eldey Island off the coast of Iceland. Actually, the cost cannot be calculated—

the birds the trio destroyed on Eldey on June 4, 1844, were the two last living great auks in the entire world.

Dodo

In 1634, Peter Mundy, an official of the British East India Company, visited Mauritius, an island lying some six hundred miles off the east coast of Africa. Mundy reported seeing "Do does, a strange kind of fowle, twice as bigge as a Goose, that can neither flye nor swymm, being Cloven footed; a wonder how it should come thither, there being none such in any part of the world yett to be found."

Four years later, Mundy's vessel again called at Mauritius. He looked vainly for "Do does" and noted in his journal, "We now mett with None."

Old print of a dodo

25

While no specimen of the dodo exists, many museums have reconstructed it. This representation, which is based on seventeenth-century paintings, has feathers taken from other birds.

Actually, the chances of Mundy's seeing a dodo in 1638 were slight. The defenseless and extremely awkward bird had proven to be easy prey for man and the animals man introduced to

Mauritius. Not only was the dodo incapable of flight but also its fastest gait was a waddle. If it tried to run, its enormous stomach scraped the ground.

The dodo was a pigeon that reached Mauritius by flying, then lost the power of flight. Before Mauritius was settled, the dodo had no enemies. Then, after man's arrival, the bird was too stupid to adjust to the change in its environment. Indeed, the dodo was so foolish that, even if it had had the ability to flee when threatened, it would have made no attempt to escape. The Portuguese who landed on Mauritius at an early date were the first to recognize the bird's lack of intelligence. This is why they called it *doudo* (simpleton), from which "dodo" is derived.

It is doubtful that any bird has a shorter recorded history than the dodo. Discovered in 1598, it was extinct by 1681, the victim of hunters, dogs, and egg-eating pigs. Unfortunately, we know practically nothing of the bird's habits, but its physical characteristics are well documented. The numerous dodoes brought to Europe between 1599 and 1666 were described by many authors and painted by court artists.

Somewhat larger than a turkey, the dodo had a massive body, weighing as much as fifty pounds. Its plumage was ashy gray, almost white on the lower breast and blackish on the thighs. A small tuft of curled feathers formed the tail, while the large head carried a nine-inch strongly hooked bill.

Even before the dodo became extinct, its bones, feathers, and skull were proudly displayed by the owners of private museums. All of these individuals envied John Tradescant, an English naturalist who had a perfect specimen in his collection. Eventually, Tradescant's zoological material—including the dodo—became the property of the Ashmolean Museum at Oxford University. While the Ashmolean is famous for being the first public museum of curiosities established in England, it is far better known for being responsible for destroying the only stuffed dodo in the world. In 1775, the curator of the Ashmolean decided that Tradescant's bird looked shabby and ordered it burned.

Huia

When the first specimens of a male and female huia *(Heteralocha acutirostris)* were sent from New Zealand to Europe, the birds were described as different species. It was a logical mistake. While both sexes had shiny black plumage and orange wattles,

The rarely flying huia of New Zealand has been extinct since 1910. Instead of flying, the huia bounded through the New Zealand forests seeking decaying logs and trees containing grubs. Specimen shown is a female.

The huia was remarkable for the way the two sexes hunted together for food. The male, bottom, would chisel a hole through the bark with his short, strong beak, and the female, top, would pull the grubs out with her long, slender bill.

their bills differed greatly. That of the male was short, nearly straight, and very sharp, while the female's bill was thin and long, and curved sharply downward.

Because of their bills, huias evolved an unique method of foraging for food as they hopped through mountain forests seeking grubs, insects, and spiders in decaying wood. The males used their bills like axes to split bark and chop out cavities as the females waited patiently. Then, after their mates excavated an insect's tunnel, the females took over and pulled the prey out with their long beaks. Few other mated birds have displayed such remarkable teamwork.

The chances are the huia might have survived if it had not preferred a life on the ground to making use of its functional wings. As a result, the birds were defenseless against cats, dogs, rats, and other introduced predators. The demands of museums for specimens of these unusual birds also hastened their extinction.

3 Flightless Land Birds

"You cannot fly without wings."—Italian Proverb

Forty-six living species of birds have lost the power of flight. These include the ostrich-like birds of the Southern Hemisphere and the penguins of frozen Antarctica which have nothing in common. Flightlessness is also found among cormorants, ducks, grebes, parrots, and rails—unrelated groups of birds, most of whose members are capable of flight. In every case, these birds stopped flying because of a lack of predatory pressure or because they developed a different type of locomotion. This is particularly true of certain rails, running birds that have colonized oceanic islands.

Rails are not the only birds to become earthbound on remote islands. Such islands were the home of most extinct flightless birds. Similarly, isolated tracts of land surrounded by a vast expanse of open sea also shelter most species of living flightless birds.

Originally, many of these islands were uninhabited and free from predators. As a result, the birds that lived on them did not have to rely upon their wings to flee danger. As the years passed, the unused wings of certain species degenerated and,

31

This flightless rail is one of the forty-six living species of birds that have lost the power to fly. The takahe lives in New Zealand.

in time, became useless. But the birds that became ground dwellers developed strong (and often long) legs.

Flightless Rails

The range of flightless birds living on islands is limited. Thus they are extremely vulnerable to man's interference with their environment. This is why seven isolated species of flightless rails

32

have become extinct in recent times. Several other species are also endangered. Cuba's zapata rail *(Cyanelimnas cerverai)* is typical of these birds. Barely capable of remaining airborne, although it has fully developed wings, *Cyanelimnas* is found only within a mile of the high ground in the forested area of the Zapata Swamp.

As its common name implies, the Inaccessible Island rail *(Atlantisia rogersi)* is not bothered by man. Famed for its strange-looking, hairlike plumage, this flightless rail is found only on the most westerly of the Tristan da Cunha Islands in the South Atlantic.

Small size is characteristic of flightless island rails, but the weka *(Gallirallus australis)* is the size of a chicken. Formerly hunted for its oil, this resident of New Zealand was once so abundant that thousands could be slaughtered in a day.

Wekas live in the forest. During most of the day they sleep in burrows under roots, emerging at dusk to feed on rats and mice. While farmers and stockmen consider the weka an ally, sportsmen regard it with mixed feelings. Besides dining on ro-

The weka, the most often seen of New Zealand's flightless birds, shows little fear of man. This flightless rail is a "pack rat"—it frequently visits camps and carries off small objects left lying around.

A South Island woodhen (weka)

dents, wekas feast on the eggs of ducks and other ground-nesting birds.

A bunch of grass tucked in a burrow or under a log serves the weka as a nest. Females usually lay four whitish, blotched eggs which they incubate for three weeks. Weka chicks are precocious—three or four days after hatching they leave the nest and join their parents as they hunt through the New Zealand night.

Kakapo

New Zealand is also the home of the kakapo *(Strigens habroptilus)*, a two-foot-long, greenish-yellow parrot that cannot fly. However, *habroptilus* does climb trees, using its rounded wings to help it hop from branch to branch and make long slides.

Because the kakapo is active at night and has an owlish appearance due to its facial disc of feathers, it was called the "owl parrot" by the Europeans who settled New Zealand. Unfortunately, the colonists did not gather a great deal of information

Despite its well-proportioned wings, the nocturnal kakapo (owl parrot) can make only downward glides of one hundred yards or more. Although once abundant, the kakapo, largest of New Zealand's six species of native parrots, is now extremely rare. As a result, its characteristic call, a series of booms during the breeding season, is being heard only infrequently in the mossy beach forests.

Incapable of true flight, the kakapo or owl parrot uses its wings when hopping from limb to limb. Although it feeds in trees, the owl parrot lives in ground burrows in small colonies.

about the kakapo's habits—once abundant, it is now on the verge of extinction.

Not only is there very little data about the kakapo but also existing descriptions of its behavior often disagree. However, it has been established that kakapos move rapidly along the forest floor by following a network of paths leading from their daytime hiding places in natural holes or burrows below roots to feeding areas in open spaces. These paths—which the birds maintain by constantly trimming any overhanging vegetation—are lined with hollows in which the birds take dust baths.

Dusting hollows and the kakapo's feeding habits reveal the presence of this extremely rare bird. Kakapos eat nectar, berries, flowers, and leaves but do not swallow any fibrous material. They extract all juice by vigorous chewing, then spit out the remaining

Painting of New Zealand's owl parrot, the kakapo

pulp in a ball. These balls provide evidence that at least one kakapo is living in any area in which they are found.

Scrubbirds

Australia's scrubbirds are extremely rare. In fact, the noisy scrubbird *(Atrichornis clamosus)* had been thought extinct for forty years. Then, in 1961, a small population was rediscovered near Two People Bay in western Australia. The bird now is known only there, although it formerly was widely distributed. Similarly, the range of the once abundant rufous scrubbird *(Atrichornis rufescens)* is becoming increasingly restricted as the rain forests of Queensland and New South Wales are cleared.

The chance that even a trained field naturalist will observe either one of these small, long-tailed, predominantly brown birds is remote. Not only does the plumage of the scrubbirds blend into the surroundings but also the two species live in dense vegetation. There they run around the forest floor feeding on insects. Occasionally they manage to flutter up to a low limb with their short, rounded, feeble wings, but their bone structure makes true flight impossible.

Despite its common name—derived from its shrill whistles—the noisy scrubbird is not only an accomplished singer with a melodious voice but also an excellent mimic of other birds' songs. Besides imitating other species, the noisy scrubbird sings duets with them. Males also include snatches of other birds' mating calls in the complicated compositions they themselves sing while courting. The rufous scrubbird also reproduces the calls and cries of other birds but its repertoire is not as extensive as that of its loud-voiced relative.

During the breeding season, males of both species engage in elaborate courtship displays. They fan their tails, draw them up and over the back, droop their stubby wings, and shake. As they quiver, the males carol their "love songs."

One of the many unusual creatures found on Madagascar, the brown mesite or roatelo is extremely rare. But the scarcity of this reluctant flyer is not its claim to fame—the roatelo is noted for not flying although it has functional wings.

Reluctant Fliers

Although capable of feeble flight, several species of birds prefer to walk or hop. Even when threatened they do not fly but instead run to safety. The pheasant coucal *(Centropus phasianius)* of New Guinea and Australia—one of the cuckoos that builds its own nest and raises its own young—forages for food in the underbrush and, when wet and cold, "climbs to the tops of bushes to spread its plumage in such a grotesque manner that it often resembles a lifeless scarecrow." If *Centropus* is disturbed while in this position, it flaps and flutters a short distance, then makes a crash landing. Once on the ground, the bird rapidly dashes to cover and hides.

The disinclination of birds to fly may, eventually, result in their wings becoming useless. There is also the possibility that, by choosing a totally terrestrial way of life, some species will be wiped out as man and his pets invade their habitat. In the last decade alone, the numbers of certain ground-dwelling birds incapable of sustained flight have been reduced greatly.

4 Flightless Seabirds

"I can swim like a fish."—Fletcher

A few species of birds have adapted to life on the water. Living in isolated regions where they can find sufficient food throughout the year and are relatively free from predators, these birds have no need to fly. As a result, their wings, unused for centuries, have gradually grown smaller and smaller.

However, although their greatly reduced wings are unable to lift these chunky birds off the water, they make excellent flippers and weapons. Flightless seabirds also use their wings when swimming and diving and to attract mates.

Cormorants

Cormorants are a large family of seabirds with representatives in most parts of the world. They are outstanding divers and swimmers. Some ornithologists claim that cormorants locate fish by sound when diving in murky water.

All thirty species of cormorants are masters of the air except the Galapagos cormorant *(Nannopeterum harrisi)*. Moreover, while its kin use their wings and webbed feet to propel them

The Galapagos cormorant, the only flightless member of a family consisting of thirty species of swimming and diving birds, waddles like a penguin when it walks.

under water, the flightless *harrisi* keeps its useless wings folded. Nor does *harrisi* stay in the water for long periods or sleep while floating as most seabirds do—its feathers do not repel water. The flightless cormorant has to go ashore frequently to dry its plumage by sitting in the sun with outstretched wings.

Three feet in length, covered with short, thick, brownish plumage that is paler on the underparts, the flightless cormorant is extremely awkward on land. The stubby, strong legs are set so far back on the body that the bird is forced to stand upright and walk with a waddle.

Ducks

Each spring and fall, vast flocks of ducks, their wings beating steadily, migrate thousands of miles to and from their nesting grounds. Some of the species that make these journeys are not only capable of long flights but also have the ability to zoom through the air at sixty miles an hour. But three of the 120 species of ducks cannot fly.

The habitat of *Tachyeres pteneres* is the source of its common name—the Magellanic flightless steamer duck. Although found in the waters of southern Chile, this bird is most numerous in the Tierra del Fuego, an archipelago south of the Strait of Magellan. A close kin, the Falkland flightless steamer duck *(Tachyeres brachypterus)*, makes its home where the cold waters of the South Atlantic lap the bleak shores of the Falkland Islands.

Steamer ducks are well named. When on the water, a steamer duck "propels itself like an old-fashioned side-wheel steamship, its wings whirling faster and faster as it gains speed." This splashing—steamer ducks have been clocked at twelve miles an hour—is apt to attract predators. Therefore the birds sink from time to time below the surface, leaving only bill and eyes above water. If danger is spotted while the flightless steamer ducks are in deep water, the birds dive deep and swim a considerable distance beneath the surface. When threatened near land, they "steam" to shore and run for cover. Incidentally, flightless steamer ducks also make frequent trips inland to drink at freshwater springs.

When spring comes to the Southern Hemisphere in October, male steamer ducks vie for nesting sites but not for the attention of females—steamer ducks mate for life. In combat, the birds beat one another with their wings and with the bill try to grab an opponent's neck so they can hold his head underwater. During these fights females may come to a drake's assistance, snorting furiously. Male steamer ducks also have a peculiar cry. It sounds just like a bullfrog!

The third species of flightless duck lives thousands of miles from the habitat of the steamer ducks. It is found on some of the Auckland Islands that lie three hundred miles south of New Zealand. Once the Auckland Island flightless duck *(Anas anas aucklandica)* was common. Today, it is found only on a few small islands.

Auckland flightless ducks not only employ their wings as "paddle wheels" but also use them as supports when clambering over the rocky shores where they hunt for insects.

Grebes

"Water witch" is the perfect nickname for any of the eighteen species of grebes distributed throughout the world. No other birds are more at home in the water. Grebes eat, sleep, court, and mate in the water and, if alarmed, sink beneath the surface without leaving a ripple to mark their disappearance. Another of their tricks is to carry their chicks piggyback underwater for several hundred yards when danger threatens. Then, before emerging, they raise their heads like periscopes and look about.

Grebes that inhabit brackish lakes, salt marshes, and coastal regions normally nest beside fresh water. In order to reach it, some species make long migrations. They usually fly by night, and in the day move on foot and by swimming, feeding as they go along. But three species of grebes do not have to travel long distances to find fresh water—they spend their entire lives in it. Slightly larger and heavier than their migrating relatives,

Painting of a flightless grebe on an Andean lake. Swallows dart above.

these birds could not leave their watery homes if they wanted to because they cannot fly.

Flightless grebes are named for the South American lakes in which they are found. Lake Junin in the Andes Mountains of Peru is the home of the Junin grebe *(Pediceps taczanowskii)*, a species on the verge of extinction. The Atitlan grebe *(Pedilymbus gigas)* is restricted to Lake Atitlan, which occupies a crater a thousand feet deep in southern Guatemala. Sprawling across the Peruvian-Bolivian border, Lake Titicaca is 12,500 feet above sea level—the highest large navigable lake in the world. Once Titicaca was the center of early South American civilization. Today, it is better known for sheltering the Titicaca grebe *(Centropelma micropterum)*.

Generally speaking, all flightless grebes share the same ways, including the habit of eating their feathers. Ornithologists theo-

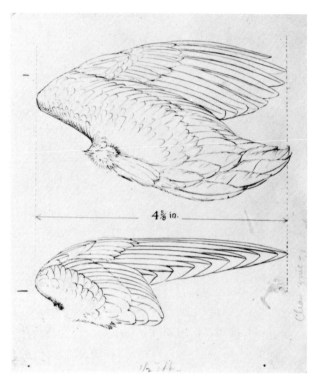

Wing of a flightless grebe, top, compared to wing of a swallow.

rize that the mat of feathers found in their stomachs acts as a buffer and prevents sharp fish bones from entering the intestines until they are soft enough to digest.

Penguins

There are seventeen species of penguins. They range from the duck-sized little blue penguin *(Eudyptula minor)* to the emperor penguin *(Aptenodytes forsteri)*, largest of flightless water birds. A mature emperor may be five feet tall and weigh nearly one hundred pounds.

Irrespective of their size, all penguins have common physical

46

characteristics. The neck and tail are short, the razor-edged bill is strong, and the stocky legs are set far back on the body. Because of the placement of the legs, penguins, like cormorants, have to stand upright and walk with a waddle.

Whether duck sized or standing waist high to a man, penguins appear husky. This is due in part to their bone structure. Most flying birds' bones are hollow, but those of penguins are solid and serve as ballast when the birds dive. Penguins have other adaptions for life in the water. When swimming, hundreds of small, hard feathers overlap like roof shingles and protect the body from cold. In addition, layers of fat under the skin provide insulation. Penguins also wear "thermal underwear"—they have thick down next to the skin.

Recognized as "the most completely aquatic of living birds,"

A curious Adélie, bottom right, approaches coastal rookery of emperor penguins.

penguins, as indicated, lost the power of flight ages ago. Over the centuries they have become excellent divers and outstanding swimmers ideally adapted for life in the water. Not only have their wings evolved into flippers but also their eyes are modified for seeing underwater.

Using their flattened, narrow wings as flippers, penguins "fly" beneath the waves, reaching speeds of fifteen miles an hour. Penguins have no fear of rough seas—certain species leap in and out of the water like porpoises. Besides using their wings to propel them through water, the birds use them as poles when they ski down icy slopes on their bellies.

All seventeen species of penguins live in the Southern Hemisphere. But, contrary to popular belief, penguins are not restricted to areas where land is snow covered and the sea is filled with drifting ice floes. Certain penguins make their home on the coast of Africa. Colonies of penguins reside on islands near the equator. Penguins are able to live in both these places because powerful currents keep the waters that wash these shores extremely cold.

Not all penguins wear black-and-white tuxedos. Several species have blue or gray plumage. Perhaps the most colorful is the king penguin *(Aptenodytes patagonica)* of the South Atlantic, which is dressed in a blue-gray jacket, bright-orange collar, and silvery-white shirt. Other penguins also have vivid collars or brilliant crests. For example, the macaroni penguin *(Eudyptes chrysolophus)* found in the southern Atlantic and Indian oceans wears a cap of flopping golden plumes.

The habits of penguins are as varied as their plumage. Some species engage in complicated courtship rites. Among these is the Adélie penguin *(Pygoscelis adeliae)* of Antarctica. Adélies trek as much as forty miles over ice to reach the rookeries where they were born to breed. These birds mate for life, and how a mated pair find one another in a colony of thousands of penguins

48

Emperor penguins "toboggan" across the Antarctic snow.

is a mystery. But they do and, before the male collects pebbles for the female to build a nest, the two face each other with upturned bills, roll their eyes down and back, raise their crests, and, with flippers held close to the sides, sway back and forth while braying so loudly they can be heard half a mile away.

Adélie guards egg in Antarctic rookery.

Adélies lay two eggs. These are incubated by the male while his mate—who has not eaten for two or three weeks—goes to sea to feed. When she returns in about twenty-one days, the male has fasted for approximately six weeks and lost half his weight. Leaving the female in charge of the eggs or the newly hatched chicks, he goes to the sea. Upon his return, both parents take care of their offspring. While one acts as a guard, the other collects food and stores it in the crop. The adult birds open their beaks and the youngsters reach in and snatch the semi-digested fish their parents regurgitate.

Two penguins that breed during the long, dark, and bitterly cold antarctic winter do not lay their eggs in nests. Nor do they deposit them on the ground. Male emperor penguins and male king penguins place the single egg laid by their mates on their feet, covering it with the tail and a loose flap of skin that hangs down from the belly. While the males incubate the eggs, the females are fishing at sea.

When female emperor penguins return to the rookery they make no attempt to find the mates that have fasted for two months. Instead, the mother bird will feed any chick that begs for food. On the other hand, mated king penguins raise their

Emperor penguin, left, and king penguin, right.

own young. Each parent cares for its offspring for about two weeks in turn.

No book the size of this one can detail all the fascinating facts learned about penguins that nest in burrows and crevices, describe the species that lay two eggs but only hatch the larger, or tell the life story of New Zealand's yellow-eyed penguin *(Megadyptes antipodes)* that spends the day sleeping in holes under rocks or roots and feeds at night. Indeed, it would take several pages to discuss the various cries of penguins. But mention must be made of the distinctive call of *Spheniscus demersus,* an inhabitant of the southern coast of Africa. This penguin sounds just like a braying donkey, which explains why it is popularly known as the jackass penguin.

5 Ratites

Birds fly by flapping their wings, which are powered by two strong muscles. One end of these muscles is fastened to the collarbone, the other end to an extension of the breastbone called the keel. Birds that possess keels are known to ornithologists as "carinates"—a word derived from the Latin *carina* (keel).

All flightless birds described in the preceding chapters have retained both the keel and the muscles that provide the mechanical energy necessary for flight. As indicated, flightless seabirds employ their wings for various purposes. As a result, their keels have not grown smaller and their flight muscles are still well developed. But the keels and flight muscles of certain species of flightless land-dwelling birds have deteriorated through disuse.

The ostrich-like birds—cassowary, emu, kiwi, ostrich, and rhea—are unique among flightless birds. These residents of the Southern Hemisphere not only have small, useless wings but also their keels and flight muscles have completely disappeared. Scientists call these birds "ratites," a name compounded from the Latin *ratis* (a raft).

53

Ratites are not a family but a group composed of five families of running birds. While these birds have certain common physical characteristics, their relationship to one another has never been established. Nor has the question of the kinship of the ratites to the tinamous—fifty species of weakly flying birds native to South America—been settled. Many authorities hold that the ratites have no close relatives. The experts also speculate whether the ostrich-like birds became ground dwellers because they grew too big to fly.

Ornithological research has revealed that, as the ratites grew larger, changes took place in their bones, muscles, and plumage. The birds' flight and tail feathers either disappeared or became transformed into decorative plumage, but the structural changes that took place enabled them to survive.

Meanwhile, ornithologists argue whether or not the ratites had a common ancestor. They also continue to debate the inter-

A flock of ostriches on a South African farm

54

relationships of living ratites, although they are willing to presume that all the ostrich-like birds are related to the extinct moa and elephant bird.

Ostriches

Most individuals have little difficulty in recognizing an ostrich *(Struthio camelus)*. The ostrich is the largest living bird, and the great length of its practically featherless neck gives it a grotesque appearance. Like the neck, its powerful thighs, small flat head (which bears a broad, shallow bill), and long legs are nearly naked.

Not only is the ostrich a well-known bird but also it is featured in two tall tales told in many lands. The first maintains that ostriches bury their heads when alarmed. There is a logical explanation for this conviction. The big birds are sensitive to the

This ostrich on her nest does not seem disturbed by tourists.

slightest noise or other disturbance when incubating their eggs and, when frightened, try to make themselves inconspicuous by lowering the head until the neck is held horizontally above the ground. Therefore, if a nest is located behind a tussock or placed in a thicket, it is almost impossible to see its occupant.

The second widespread notion about the ostrich holds that it will "eat almost anything including lumps of metal and tins of paint." Actually, there is considerable truth to this belief.

56

Not only do ostriches avidly swallow small shiny objects but also they have the ability to digest metal. The latter, along with the other coarse materials the birds eat, is first softened by gastric juices, then ground down by stones in the gizzard. These stones are gulped down by baby ostriches shortly after hatching. Digestion is also aided by the sand that adult birds ingest from time to time.

Fossils reveal that nine species of ostrich inhabited southern Europe, the Middle East, and Asia eons ago. Today, one species survives, but it too has become extinct or rare over much of its former range. Once a common sight in much of Africa, Syria, and Saudi Arabia, the bird is now plentiful only in the sandy grasslands and thornbush country of East Africa. The ostriches that roam the Australian outback are the descendants of birds that were imported in the nineteenth century and reared there

This illustration from a Victorian children's book furthered the tall tale about ostriches hiding their heads.

Main house of Highgate Ostrich Farm, Oudtshoorn, South Africa

in captivity to provide plumes for the hats and fans of fashionable ladies.

Ornithologists have divided the surviving species of ostrich into several races. Identification is made by the reddish or bluish skin on the neck and thighs. In all races the males are approximately seven to eight feet tall and weigh about three hundred pounds. Females are much smaller, and their grayish-brown plumage is dull and unattractive compared to that of the males. The latter have body feathers that are a brillant black, while the short wing plumes and the tail are pure white.

Perhaps the most unique physical characteristic of the ostrich is the feet. Ostriches have two toes per foot—all other birds have three or four. Both toes are tipped with extremely sharp nails, and one toe is considerably larger than the other. Ostriches attack enemies with their feet, striking right and left, the razor-like nails ripping a foe's flesh to shreds. However, ostriches would rather retreat than fight. With their long powerful legs, they can cover fifteen feet in a single stride and maintain a speed of forty miles an hour for thirty minutes. If the ostrich did not have the habit of running in great circles, "a man on horseback would rarely get a shot at it."

Not only do their sharp nails, alertness, and speed protect ostriches from man and animal predators but so do their acute hearing and exceptionally keen vision. Ostriches *should* have outstanding eyesight—their eyeballs are about the size of tennis balls!

Cautious creatures, ostriches avoid forested areas and keep to open country where their long necks and excellent vision enable them to detect distant danger. As a result, zebras and

The ancient Romans employed ostriches to draw chariots. Today, jockeys race the birds in South Africa.

Male ostrich displays spectacular plumage.

various species of antelope frequently associate with these birds, which act as "watchdogs" for the animals. The ostriches also benefit—they dine on the insects, reptiles, and rodents flushed by the hoofs of the grazing zebra and antelope.

Although the omnivorous ostrich enjoys the snacks furnished by its four-footed associates, its staple diet consists of fruits, seeds, and grasses. Ostriches can go without water for days—in dry regions their thirst is satisfied by the juices of succulent plants—but they enjoy frequent drinks. They also delight in bathing—always keeping the neck and head above the surface.

At the start of the breeding season, males display their plumes, establish territories, and woo mates with elaborate courtship ceremonies. Although monogamy is not unknown among ostriches, males usually are polygamous, having three to five hens in their harems. Females leave both the selection of the nest site and the making of the nest to their mates. Nests are constructed by scraping out a shallow depression in the ground that may be nearly ten feet across. The cavity has to be large. Not only

Old print of a female ostrich shows her duller plumage. Note the sharply clawed, two-toed feet.

On South African ostrich farms the birds make their nests beneath man-made shelters designed to shield the eggs from the heat of the sun.

Ostrich eggs and hatchling. Note other chicks struggling to emerge.

does every member of a harem deposit eggs in it but also¹ each hen may lay as many as twenty straw-yellow or buff-colored shiny eggs that are approximately seven inches long. Compared to the average chicken egg, which weighs slightly more than two ounces, ostrich eggs are tremendous. They weigh about three pounds each.

It may take three weeks for all the hens to lay their eggs. After all the eggs have been placed in the nest, the dominant female drives the other hens away and broods the entire clutch. This is very unusual. In all other ratite species the males do the incubating. Actually, the dominant ostrich female only broods during the day when her drab plumage blends with the surrounding terrain. The male takes over the task at night when his brilliant feathers cannot call a predator's attention to the nest.

Emu

When Europeans first settled Australia, the mainland and several nearby islands were inhabited by various species of emu. Today only one species survives *(Dromains novahollandiae)*. Approximately six feet tall, it is the second-largest living bird.

This sole surviving species of emu lives on the Australian mainland. It has the same type of plumage as its extinct kin. Emus have double feathers whose barbs are so widely separated that they do not interlock to form the stiff vane found in the feathers of most modern birds. As a result, emus wear a loose, downy coat. Because the barbs on the feathers that extend from the back near the base of the spine remain unlinked, they droop and form the moplike "tail."

The long unfeathered legs bear three toes whose undersides are flattened into a broad pad. When chased, emus can reach speeds up to forty miles an hour while taking nine-foot strides. Besides being swift runners, emus also swim well.

Emus at the Tidbinbilla Fauna Reserve near Canberra, national capital of Australia, will always welcome a visitor who brings food.

Until comparatively recent times, emus were found throughout the Australian mainland. Tremendous herds made seasonal migrations across the countryside seeking fruits, flowers, insects, seeds, and green vegetation, (Emus eat dried herbage and the leaves of shrubs only during prolonged droughts).

Although the vast numbers of migrating emu ate untold millions of beetles, caterpillars, and grasshoppers as well as consuming tons of the burrs that catch on sheep's wool during their cross-country treks, cattlemen, farmers, and sheepmen did not consider them as allies. The birds competed with cattle and sheep for grass, drank at the watering tanks built for stock in arid regions, broke fences, and caused tremendous economic loss to those who raised wheat in Western Australia.

In the 1930's, the government placed a fifty-cent bounty on the emu. Thousands of the birds were slaughtered. But still they flourished. Finally, in 1932, the authorities declared an all out war on the birds. They ordered a company of the Royal Australian Artillery—equipped with two machine guns and ten thousand shells—into the field to decimate the emus. The plan was to drive them along fences until they were within range—a tactic that had proven successful in the state of New South Wales. But the operation in Western Australia was a military disaster. Only twelve birds were killed. Not only did the emus outwit the soldiers by breaking up into small bands but also the machine guns jammed at the one time great numbers of birds were in point-blank range.

Because of these mishaps, the offensive, known to Australians as the "Great Emu War," came to a sudden end. Some thirty years later, the government of Western Australia was still paying a bounty on emus. Eventually it was decided not to attempt to exterminate them but rather to confine them to the northern part of the state. To limit the movement of the emus and to protect the wheatlands and sheep farms in the southwest from an invasion, an emu-proof fence some five hundred miles long was erected and wardens were assigned to patrol it.

Meanwhile, ranchers and farmers continued to shoot and poison emus and to smash their eggs. This, plus the inroads of civilization, drastically reduced the size of the herds. Fearful that the emu might become extinct, the Australian government established sanctuaries where the birds could breed unmolested.

Because the emu thrives in these sanctuaries and also readily breeds in captivity, there is little danger of its becoming an endangered species at the present time, even though the birds are still treated as pests on their natural range.

Emu nests of grass, leaves, and twigs are usually located under a tree or bush, being placed so that the view in all directions

Although the emu is depicted on Australia's coat of arms, many farmers "Down Under" consider the bird a pest because of the damage it does to their crops.

Old print of emu with young

is unobstructed. Males build the nests, incubate the eggs, and care for the chicks. They rarely leave a nest until their young hatch. If they do, they cover the nest with leaves. While incubating, the males seldom eat and never drink.

Kiwi

Kiwis, the national symbol of New Zealand, are restricted to that country. Because they have little in common with other ratites, some authorities theorize that kiwis are "living fossils"—

The kiwi lacks a tail and has no visible wings. Note the sharply clawed toes, the coat of hairlike feathers, and the enormous egg.

miniature moas that have managed to survive to the present day.

The kiwi has been called the most unbirdlike of birds. One reason is that its two-inch-long wings cannot be seen. They lie under a mat of gray or brown hairlike feathers that cover the entire body, with the exception of two bare spots on the sides. All three kiwi species have the same form but vary slightly in size. About as large as a domestic fowl, the tailless kiwis weigh between three and nine pounds. The rounded body is carried on short stocky legs that bear three sharply clawed toes. Although their gait is extremely awkward—one foot being placed directly in front of the other—a kiwi can outrun a man.

68

Kiwis have poor daylight vision but they see well with their small eyes when foraging for food at night. Large ear openings and acute hearing enable the birds to detect prowling predators and other dangers. But the kiwi's most sensitive sensory organ is its nose. Not only are kiwis the only living birds with a well-developed sense of smell but also they differ from all other birds in having the nostril openings near the tip of the bill. The long bristles at the base of the long slender bill are thought to be organs of touch.

Kiwis inhabit damp pine forests. During the daylight hours they remain in deep burrows that may contain several chambers. When dusk falls, the birds leave their hideouts, which are usually surrounded by thick vegetation, to feed.

Observation has revealed that a kiwi constantly taps the ground with its bill in much the same fashion that a blind individual uses a cane. But the bird is not using the bill as a crutch— it is trying to detect the scent of insects or earthworms. When its keen sense of smell picks up the presence of buried food, a

Young kiwi probes the ground for insects. It will use its long bill to pry out its food.

kiwi drives its bill into the earth with the strong muscles of the short, thick neck, then uses the bill like a crowbar to pry up its prey.

Until comparatively recent times, thousands of kiwis were killed and their feathers made into trout flies that were highly prized by fisherman. Meanwhile, the birds were being preyed upon by cats, dogs, foxes, and the other animals that settlers introduced into New Zealand. Besides upsetting the balance of nature, man also reduced the kiwi's range by opening more and more land to farming and stock raising.

Despite the activities of man and animals, the kiwi managed to survive, due to its alertness, nocturnal habits, and the ability to defend itself by kicking forward and slashing a foe with its sharp claws. However, in time, the kiwi population dropped rapidly. New Zealanders—who are so fond of the bird that as well as employing it as their national symbol place its picture on money and stamps and also call members of New Zealand's armed forces "kiwis"—became alarmed.

In 1921, because of the concern of conservationists, the government established kiwi sanctuaries and enacted strict laws controlling the export of kiwis. Today, despite the pressure of introduced predators and the reduction of its natural habitat, the kiwi is in no danger of becoming extinct.

Female kiwis usually lay only one chalky-white, thin-shelled egg but clutches of two or three are not unknown. Considering a kiwi's size, the eggs are enormous. About five inches long, they may weigh eighteen ounces. This is approximately one-eighth the weight of the female. Therefore, kiwi eggs are the world's largest in proportion to the size of the bird that lays them. If evaluated by the same standard, ostrich eggs are the smallest eggs laid by any living bird.

Males do all the incubating, which takes from eight to eleven weeks, depending upon the species. The eggs are rarely left

In proportion to its size, the kiwi lays the largest egg of any bird. It is about four times larger than the eggs of other birds of similar size.

unattended, the male remaining on the nest for days without water or food. Sometimes, after a chick hatches, a female may deposit another egg in the nest. The weary male does not protest and immediately starts to incubate the egg.

Cassowaries

Few birds have a worse reputation than the cassowary. Both tribal tale-tellers and scientific writings have long maintained that these flightless residents of the rain forests of New Guinea,

71

Native to the coastal swamp forests of New Guinea and adjacent islands, the single-wattled cassowary stands four feet tall and weighs up to 128 pounds. Its single short wattle hangs from the throat, while the two long wattles of the double-wattled cassowary hang from the neck.

the adjacent islands, and the northeastern coast of Queensland are the only birds capable of killing a man with a single blow. However, the cassowary's notoriety may be unjustified. While rumors of deaths caused by cassowaries are constantly heard in regions where the birds occur, confirmed reports of actual casualties are lacking. However, there are records of zoo attendants and New Guinea tribesmen being injured by cassowaries.

There are three species of cassowaries and nineteen subspecies whose true distribution has been established by zoologists. The largest of the group is the one-wattled cassowary *(Casuarius unappendiculatus)*, which stands about four feet tall. The dwarf cassowary *(Casuarius bennetti)*, as its common name implies, is the smallest. *Bennetti* is slightly over three feet in height.

Cassowaries have an eye-catching appearance. One reason is the flattened, bony, helmet-like crest—technically called a casque—that projects some six inches above the skull. But the wattles—folds of skin on the throat—are far more colorful. Their hues range from vivid blues, garish greens, gaudy oranges, flashy purples, and showy reds to yellows that one naturalist has described as "sickening." Ornithologists distinguish the various species by the wattles' form and the helmet's shape. For example, the Australian cassowary *(Casuarius casuarius)* wears a helmet that rises high above the head and has two folds of skin on its neck. These folds are the source of its popular name—the two-wattled cassowary.

Not only does the dwarf cassowary lack wattles but also its silklike plumage is duller than the almost black, glossy-textured, bristle-like plumage of its larger kin. The cassowary has the same type of feathers as the emu. Because they do not interlock, the feathers hang loosely from the body and resemble hair.

Despite their size, powerful legs, and wickedly sharp middle toes, cassowaries are exceptionally shy and wary. Moveover, they are solitary, the sexes joining together only during the breeding

73

season. Thus cassowaries are seldom seen as they wander through the forests during the early morning or late afternoon seeking food. While the Australian cassowary feeds mainly on wild and cultivated fruits, it—like other cassowaries—will dine on insects and vegetation when its regular menu is not available.

More often heard than seen—cassowary calls are similar to those of the emu—these secretive birds remain hidden when not foraging. When they are surprised in the open, cassowaries dash for cover along well-worn runs. But even if no run is nearby, a frightened cassowary is not handicapped. It can move at speeds of thirty miles an hour through dense undergrowth, thorny bushes, and entangling vines. While running, the head—protected by the bony casque—is held down and forward while the sturdy wing quills are held outward. The quills serve as shields and turn aside sharp-edged leaves and thorns as the bird slides between obstructions, leaps over barriers—a cassowary can clear a five-foot fence—and rushes to the nearest body of water, where it plunges in and swims rapidly to the opposite shore.

Cassowaries don't dive into water only when they are threatened. They frequently enter a stream to take a refreshing bath and a swim. In reporting the cassowary's fondness for swimming, E. Thomas Gilliard, a noted field ornithologist, suggests that, with the helmet and the naked, wattled, garishly colored neck, "a swimming cassowary presents a frightening spectacle to the uninitiated."

Mated cassowaries establish and defend a territory in which they build a nest consisting of a shallow depression lined with a mat of grass. As soon as the female finishes laying three to eight eggs her mate begins to incubate them. It takes seven to eight weeks for the eggs to hatch. When the chicks emerge, the male takes charge of them, just as he incubated the eggs, alone.

When hatched, the chicks have a yellow-brown plumage barred with a pattern of light- and dark-brown longitudinal stripes that blends into the surroundings.

Despite their camouflage, cassowary chicks are often caught by New Guinea tribesmen who have hunted the birds for hundreds of years. Besides eating cassowary hearts ceremoniously, native hunters have long feasted on the birds' flesh (they are particularly fond of the liver). They also use the feathers for ornamentation and for barter. As a result, any cassowary chicks that are captured and not eaten are treated as pets and allowed to roam freely through the villages. But when the downy coats of these "domesticated" chicks give way to brown plumage—the sign of approaching maturity—the birds are placed in cages.

In some instances a cassowary will spend the rest of its life in a cage, the owner plucking its plumes regularly. Other birds are kept in extremely small cages where movement is restricted. There they are fattened until they are killed and eaten. Still others are sold to animal dealers. E. T. Gilliard, an authority on the birds of the Australasian region, writes that a Papuan—a resident of the southwest section of New Guinea—can make enough money selling a cassowary to buy either eight large pigs or a wife!

Rheas

Zoologists named the rhea after the mother of Zeus, supreme god of the ancient Greeks. But the nickname of the New World's largest bird has nothing to do with Greek mythology. To ornithologists and laymen alike, the rhea is known as the "South American ostrich."

Despite this nickname, the rhea does not belong to the same family of birds as the ostrich. Nevertheless, at first glance, these two ratites look alike. But closer examination reveals that they differ in many respects. Rheas stand five feet high and weigh about fifty pounds—ostriches are considerably taller and heavier. Moreover, male ostriches have white plumes in the wings and tail. Not only do rheas lack tails but also their wings—which are much larger than the wings of other ratities—have no plumes.

A few hairlike feathers are scattered over the practically naked head and neck of the rhea. There are no feathers near the eyes, bill, and ears. However, the ears are surrounded by fine bristles. The rest of the body is covered with soft, floppy plumage. Because rhea feathers have little commercial value, the birds have not suffered at the hands of man. But large carnivores eat adult rheas, while birds of prey take the young.

Predators have difficulty stalking rheas. The acute hearing and excellent eyesight of the birds enable them to detect potential danger when it is far away. If surprised and forced to flee, rheas take five-foot strides on their long, powerful legs that have three front toes but no hind toe.

There are two species of rhea. The more abundant of the two, the common rhea *(Rhea americana)* is found on the pampas of Argentina and Brazil. Highlands from southern Peru to Patagonia is the habitat of the smaller Darwin's rhea *(Pterocnemia pennata)*. In both species, males and females present a similar appearance. However, generally speaking, male common rheas are larger than females.

As indicated, the fast-running rheas live in open country. Therefore it is logical to assume that their first reaction to danger is to flee from it. But if dense vegetation provides cover, the birds will crouch and hide rather than run away. When discovered, they dash off, necks held horizontally. Rheas dodge obstacles with ease. They make sudden changes in direction by raising one wing and lowering the other, just as a pilot steers an airplane by changing the position of its rudders.

Rheas are gregarious. Not only do they live in flocks that may

Most of the common rheas that range from northeastern Brazil to central Argentina have gray-brown plumage with white tail feathers. However, white specimens are frequently seen. Rheas are the biggest birds in the New World.

number fifty birds but also they like to associate with bush deer, cattle, and guanacos. Incidentally, the introduction of cattle and horses into South America changed the traditional method of hunting rheas—encircling a flock. Today, *vaqueros* chase rheas on horseback and bring them down with bolas—three stone balls attached to heavy cords.

Excellent swimmers, rheas often dwell near swamps or rivers. But they drink very little water, satisfying their thirst with plant juices. Besides eating grasses, leaves, roots, seeds, and other vegetation, rheas consume insects, lizards, snails, slugs, worms, and various small mammals. The birds also have the habit of gobbling down any small shiny object.

Although rheas do not migrate, they wander considerable distances searching for food. During their travels, the flocks stay more or less together, except for the old males who lead solitary lives. During the breeding season—September to December— the flocks break up as the males seek mates.

Once a male rhea establishes a territory, he zealously defends it. No other male is allowed to come near. Captive birds even drive the keepers away. In order to discourage a trespassing bird, males assume a threatening posture which consists of facing the intruder with the neck lowered into a U-shape. If this display fails to intimidate the unwanted visitor, the rivals fight. It is a bloody contest, the combatants biting and kicking each other while their necks are entwined. When one male breaks away, he is chased by the winner, who advertises his triumph by spreading his wings and holding the neck in an S-curve.

Rheas are polygamous. A male may have a harem of six to eight hens. In order to attract females, the males fluff up their feathers, run in all directions with the neck outstretched and swinging from side to side, and cry *nan-du* in a deep voice. This cry sounds more like the roar of a large mammal than

Old print of a rhea. The bird was often referred to as a nandu because of its call.

the call of a bird. Males finish their courtship display by drawing close to a female, lowering the neck, and dropping to the ground. If a female responds to this wooing, the birds mate.

The male builds the nest, which is merely a scrape in the ground some three feet across and one foot deep lined with a few bits of vegetation. The site of the nest is usually concealed, and field naturalists report that the birds clear away the grass and bushes surrounding it. Some authorities claim that the birds are instinctively making a firebreak.

The most unusual thing about rhea eggs is that they undergo a color change during incubation. The common rhea's elliptical, shiny, ivory or golden-yellow eggs gradually become paler. Similarly, the yellowish-green eggs of Darwin's rhea fade to a washed-out yellow. The eggs of both species—which have a volume equal to that of twelve chicken eggs—are eaten by South Americans, although most individuals dislike the taste of rhea meat.

Females lay between ten and twenty eggs each. Some do not wait for a nest to be excavated but deposit their eggs on the bare ground. Nevertheless, the average nest holds a large number of eggs. This is because all the hens in a harem use the same nest. Thus the male—who does all the incubating—may be called upon to brood as many as eighty eggs. As it is impossible for a male to cover a clutch of more than twenty or thirty eggs, all the rest, along with those that were laid outside the nest, are wasted. The brooded eggs hatch in thirty-five to forty days.

Male rheas also assume full responsibility for rearing the chicks. The youngsters, dressed in yellowish-gray downy coats barred with black longitudinal stripes, are well camouflaged as they follow their parents about. Adults and chicks keep contact with one another by mournful whistles, but this does not prevent chicks from becoming lost. When this happens, the chick joins the first family group it encounters. As a result, a male rhea often has charge of birds of different ages.

Despite their protective coloring and the care given to them by their fathers or foster-fathers, many rhea chicks provide predators with a feast. Those that survive mature in about six months.

6 Conservation or Extinction?

"The future is hidden from all men."—Demosthenes

In recent years, tribesmen in remote areas once known only to explorers and missionaries have become familiar with the chain saw's whine and the bulldozer's roar. On every continent, forests are being felled, streams dammed, and swamps drained because of the demand for more land on which to produce food for the Earth's ever increasing population. As a result, thousands of square miles formerly inhabited by various forms of wildlife are now used for farming or for stock raising.

Many individuals who know what man's interference did to the great auk, the dodo, and the moa are concerned that "progress" will bring about the extermination of numerous groups of living birds. This is due to the fact that many species are adapted for life in a specific habitat and, if that habitat is destroyed, they cannot survive. Fortunately, despite man's transformation of their environment, the future of most species of ratite birds is assured. Not only are the majority of species protected by strictly enforced laws but also adequate refuges have been provided where they can raise their young. Then, too, nearly all the ratites breed freely in captivity.

Believed extinct for over fifty years, the takahe (Notornis mantelli) *was redis-covered in a remote New Zealand valley in 1948. However, hardly more than 300 specimens exist of this flightless rail that lays two eggs but hatches only one. Not only is the takahe one of the world's rarest birds but also it is one of the most beautiful. The head, neck, and breast are bright blue, the back and wing feathers olive green, and the frontal plate, bill, and feet are red.*

Some twenty years ago the New Zealand government set out to raise the takahe in captivity. The experiment was unsuccessful for twenty years. Then, in 1977, the first chicks were reared to maturity.

ABOVE: *Takahe hen feeding the first takahe chick born in captivity at the Mount Bruce Native Bird Reserve near Wellington, the capital city of New Zealand.*

Maturing takahe chick being examined by conservation officer

Flightless and brilliantly colored, the takahe is the size of a big rooster.

But the future of many flightless birds is not as bright as that of the ratites. Conservationists pose questions whose answers lie far in the future. Among the things individuals who enjoy wildlife would like to know are: Will oil slicks wipe out flightless steamer ducks? Does the exploitation of natural resources hidden beneath the everlasting snows of Antarctica mean the end of the penguin? Will the owl parrot vanish because of the world's need for lumber?

Generally speaking, flightless birds are unable to adapt to changes in their environment. They are overspecialized and their restricted way of life permits no variation of behavior. This means that the extinction of the majority of flightless birds in the wild is inevitable if man continues to encroach upon feeding and nesting grounds.

Humans have short memories. Not too long ago millions of migrating passenger pigeons darkened the skies of North America. Untold numbers of these birds were slaughtered by market hunters until only one specimen was left—and it died in the Cincinnati Zoo in 1914. Although more and more people are recognizing that many species of birds—particularly those that cannot fly—are apt to follow the passenger pigeon into oblivion, sixteen species of flightless birds have disappeared in recent years. None became extinct because of ecological changes. All of them were the victims of "progress." For example, certain rails native to oceanic island vanished as a result of their habitat's being destroyed to make landing fields for aircraft.

Today, the world's ever-growing population becomes increasingly dangerous to flightless birds. To remove the threat to these species, we must do two things. First, suitable habitat must be set aside and provided with the protection needed to maintain numbers of various flightless birds. Secondly, so far as the more endangered species are concerned, experiments in rearing them in captivity should be undertaken and young birds released into the wild.

Obviously, successfully raising certain flightless birds in captivity will be no easy task. But if only one species is saved from extinction, it will be well worth the effort. After all, we have "come a long way from the time when man's chief interest in birds was to eat them."

Index

88